SECRETS OF MARKETING TO MOMS

Judy Peterson

Peterson Publishing & Media

Copyright © 2020 Peterson Publishing

All rights reserved

The characters and events portrayed in this book are fictitious. Any similarity to real persons, living or dead, is coincidental and not intended by the author.

No part of this book may be reproduced, or stored in a retrieval system, or transmitted in any form or by any means, electronic, mechanical, photocopying, recording, or otherwise, without express written permission of the publisher.

ISBN-13: 9798651797301
ISBN-10: 1477123456

Cover design by: Art Painter
Library of Congress Control Number: 2018675309
Printed in the United States of America

❊ ❊ ❊

This book is dedicated to all of my clients and my family who have supported me working from home and serving moms for the past 21 years.

❊ ❊ ❊

Mission:
Helping businesses scale up strong by using their website, events and marketing techniques/tools.

CONTENTS

Table of Contents - 5
Introduction - 6
Secret #1 Moms are Your Ideal Customer - 7
Secret #2 Not All Moms are Alike - 9
Secret #3 Where Do You Find Moms - 12
Secret #4 Moms on Facebook - 15
Secret #5 Moms on Instagram - 18
Secret #6 Moms on Pinterest - 21
Secret #7 Moms on TikTok - 23
Secret #8 Moms and Emails - 25
Secret #9 Mom Loyalty Programs - 29
Secret #10 Events for Moms - 33
Secret #11 Mom Groups, Print and Other Options - 36
Secret #12 Enticements and Offers for Moms - 40
Secret #13 Moms and Your Website - 43
Secret #14 The Mom Market and Your Brand - 46

INTRODUCTION

My name is Judy Peterson. When I first became a mom, I started to really study how they gathered and what habits they had. For 20 years I published a free printed magazine for moms in Corpus Christi, Texas. I ran this and another mom oriented directory. I started it when my oldest child was born and sold it when my youngest was graduating. During that time I learned a lot about the mom marketplace and worked with hundreds of businesses to market their brands to the moms in the local area.

This book is the result of all of the knowledge I learned during that time. I have seen businesses thrive and die in that mom market, I would love to be able to help your business be successful. Please take the information in this book, apply it to your brand, serve moms and be profitable.

SECRET #1

Moms are your ideal customer

If moms are your ideal customer, you have made a good choice. When they have a child is one time in a mom's life that they are willing to spend a lot of money. Often they will sacrifice their own wants and needs to give their children the best.

There are many opportunities to provide products and services to moms over the lifetime of their children. For the purposes of this book we will mostly consider moms of children up to age 12-13 as the target for this marketplace.

The mom market really starts even before the child is born. Maternity clothes, baby showers, strollers and wardrobe are some of the things new parents feel are needed. These parents, their families and friends are willing to invest in the best. I have even seen moms go out and buy new cars to hold their precious cargo.

Over the lifetime of a child there are different stages. Some stages are fleeting, like pregnancy and the first year, and others last the whole childhood. Moms will need to feed, clothe and entertain the child for their whole childhood, though all of these will take different forms as the child ages.

What I am trying to say is that there are many ways to segment the mom market just by paying attention to what age their children are. They can also be separated by the age of the moms. I will be covering that and other differences in the next chapter.

Saying that "moms" are your ideal customer is not enough. You have to take a look at all of the different attributes moms have and decide which are the best fit for your brand. You may find that all moms may or may not really be a great fit. If that is so you will want to define who exactly you want to market to and be intentional about who you target, what copy you create and where you decide to put your marketing dollars.

I know you can benefit from the knowledge I have gathered over the years, and I have tried to make this book a relevant guide to how you can get that done.

SECRET #2

All Moms are Not the Same

Merriam Webster® defines <u>Mom as</u> <u>a female parent : Mother</u>

Pretty much it just means you have kids. It includes birth moms, step moms and adoptive moms. Moms of babies (ages 0-1), toddlers (ages 1-2), pre-schoolers (ages 2-5), elementary age kids (ages 5-9) and tweens (ages 9-12). We will stop there for the purposes of this book.

Moms have many different lifestyle choices. Most put their children in either a public or private school when they get to be around 5 or 6. Some choose to homeschool. Many put their children in pre-school or utilize a day care for the little ones' or even just need after school care.

Some moms work outside of the home, some work a business at their home and some are stay at home moms. Do not be fooled though, all moms work. They work their butts off taking care of their children. Even if they have help most moms at a minimum clean, cook and chauffeur.

A large percentage of moms these days are single moms too. For whatever reason they are raising the children on their own and often these moms work outside of the home too. These moms look especially for convenience and time savers.

Beliefs are another thing that separate moms. Some are traditional beliefs, some are religious and some are not. Some be-

liefs have to do with diet, healthcare and behavior and some of these are very staunchly held and voiced.
Examples of these would be strong opinions on vaccines, organic foods, education, hobbies and different religious beliefs.

Other beliefs have to do with activities. There are "sports moms", "dance moms", moms that are outdoorsy, academically oriented and moms that are all about music.

Some moms celebrate holidays and birthdays in a very big way. Others put more emphasis and invest more in lessons for their kids. Some have lots of disposable income and some don't.

Then there are the age differences. Moms can be very young – teens. Or very old - grandmothers are sometimes raising their grandkids as a surrogate mom. Most moms fall between the ages of 20 and 45. The young moms usually have younger children, and if the older moms have young ones, it is usually because they have had multiple children or it is a God given blessing to a couple that had trouble having children, or perhaps even adopted children. The moms with small children at an older age seem to act more like the younger moms. Kids seem to keep you younger – maybe because they will keep you on your toes.

> These differences are all factors that you should keep in mind when you are choosing your marketing to moms platforms, messaging and targeting. We will be discussing how to do some of that in the next couple of chapters. You should sit down, take a look at the types of moms that will be most interested in your brand and come up with a few "mom profiles" that match your ideal customer profile.

There was a meme circulating a while back that is amusing and has a bit of truth to it as well.

Here it is:

SECRET #2

Moms that you might know:

Sharon
- Has a Starbucks card
- Tries to hard to be cool
- Enjoys swing chairs

Susan
- Runs a "Homelife" blog
- Facebook mom
- Makes great quinoa

Pam
- Still shops in the Juniors section
- Always has snacks on the counter
- Drives a mini van with movie screens

Jillian
- Has 50 kids
- Just wants to take a nap
- Likes the house set at 9000 degrees

Carol
- Uses terms like "blood orange"
- PTA Mom
- Is the saltiest of the suburban moms

Helen
- Neighborhood Association President
- Is sick of your kid's crap
- Will fight you

Rikki
- Hates mini vans and cooking
- Eats her kid's candy then helps look for it later
- Loves her own kids, but not crazy about other people's kids

Lynne
- Drinks beer and black coffee, not wine, kombucha or sweet tea
- Has dance parties with her kid to Devo & Skrillex
- When child asks "Do spiders poop?" says "I don't know kiddo" and whips out her phone

SECRET #3

Where do you find moms?

Moms tend to gather in groups. Most of the time if you look for the kids, you will find a group of moms socializing somewhere nearby. Parks, playgrounds of schools, athletic fields, festivals and waiting rooms for lessons.

One place that is a huge gathering and takes lots of time daily for many moms is the pickup line at any school. This is a place that moms gather, but in their own vehicles and really have nothing going on but waiting for their children to appear and get into the car to go home or to another activity. If you can reach moms in this line you have a good chance of catching her full attention. Some of the ways I have seen this done is by bus bench ads, social media posts and text messaging.

Another place that moms spend a lot of time waiting is in waiting rooms. Doctors, dentists, lessons, salons and auto repair locations all require time to be spent with no real requirements, except to wait. For many years these were great places to leave magazines or other printed materials. In the past 3 years, while it can still be useful to put them there, the majority of especially younger moms never look at them, but stay focused on their phones instead. That means that you must use online methods as well as print to be most effective.

Moms tend to have their circles of influence, much like the circles we all saw in high school. Not necessarily click-ish, but some are. Mostly they gather by ages and hobbies of the children. Moms of small children tend to have "playgroups" that gather weekly or sometimes more often than than that. Once children enter elementary school the moms are sorted more into groups where the child is involved in an activity such as dance, scouts, soccer or by school activities. As the kids get older this becomes more pronounced as the kids enter more competitive situations. Parents are expected to hang around, wait and supervise until the kids get to be in high school and can drive themselves.

These waiting times are some of the best places to reach moms if you can find a way to do it. During these times you will also find that moms spend their time talking to other moms. That is why word of mouth and "viral" is so important in mom circles. You want to have mom advocates to share their great experiences with other moms if at all possible, that alone can really grow your brand. Going "viral" is the way you get the moms talking about you in the first place. Do something fun that they can look forward to and invite their mom friends or even contests. We will talk more about contests in our next chapter.

Moms are very social. They love groups where they can meet up and if they can't leave the house to meet up they will gather in groups on social media. This is why it is very important to have mom "fans" and "followers" for your brand, they will pass the word on to other moms without you even trying to get them to do it.

For instance: Say one mom in a group of moms has a birthday party with ponies and their child loves it. Other children will probably love it too. Then other moms in the group will want to have pony parties. It usually spreads through the whole group, sometimes a whole school. Some moms may love it so much they have one several years in a row. Then, if you have other types of parties they may call you year after year and every year recommend you to other friends. Mom to mom referrals are gold. They may not be enough to support your business year round, but they create loyal customers and you need to have them and treat them well.

Mom groups are very prevalent and great places to find moms, but you must also work other channels. Let's look at some social media tactics in the next few chapters.

SECRET #4

Moms on Facebook®

Facebook® is one of the very best places to find mom groups. There are tons of them there, but the only problem is that most do not allow you to solicit for any businesses. You can join them and be active so that people start to see your name, but you do not want to make the admins mad at you. Some of them will allow you to pay them to put posts in the group promoting your brands. Be sure to read all of the rules and contact the admins if you have questions.

You will definitely want to create a business page and maybe even a group page. How do you get followers to your page? Start with your friends and clients. Ask them to share your page. Contests are an excellent way to draw more people to your page. Photo contests of cute kids, sweepstakes for prizes, and even coloring contests tend to work fairly well to get new people to like your page.

You can use your page to get moms to sign up for a group too. Groups are a way to get moms talking to each other and since you own the group you can set the rules. I would advise if you make a group that you not allow the network marketer moms to take it over. Moms don't like to be always getting ads from anyone and unfortunately some network marketing moms do not know where to draw that line.

Don't get me wrong, I love network marketing, but there are a lot of moms that do it and that in combination with some being overzealous can drive people away from your page. One solution to this is doing a "marketing Monday" or something along the lines of posting one time a week and letting everyone put their businesses on that single thread. The business owner moms will appreciate this and no one will be angry that they get ads all the time.

Be sure to post several times a week with interesting information (not ads) on both your business page and group to get the best response. You can hold your contests on the business page and use the group page to drive traffic to the contest. Don't forget to post during the times that moms are sitting in the pickup line at the schools if that is your target.

A really good place to promote your brand to moms is also the "Trash to Treasure" or "Garage Sale" groups on Facebook®. Many many moms are members of these groups and the sole purpose of them is to advertise products and services. Some have strict rules for businesses and some don't so be sure to read the rules if you decide to post in any of these groups.

Don't forget to use hashtags on your posts too. This is not as important on Facebook® as it is in other social media formats, but it is a good way to mark posts so that you can find them later. Hashtags if you don't know are keywords that use a # before them. So for example #markettomoms would be a hashtag we might use when publicizing for this book.

Hashtags make the content that they are attached to searchable. Find something that works for your brand or use a hashtag that is trending to help you reach more people.

Facebook® advertising is a fantastic way to reach moms. Unfortunately this can be very complicated, and there may be a bit of a learning curve to get it right and not waste a bunch of money. Decide how much you are willing to spend, come up with an offer (we will talk more about this in chapter 10) and decide who your ideal customer is so that you can target effectively.

Stay away from "promoting posts", it is not as effective for most promotions. It does work ok for promoting a contest on your page, but regular Facebook® ads are the most effective and economic way to promote your brand overall.

If you are interested in running Facebook® ads, it is often most economical to hire someone to help run them you or even do them for you. They can be very time consuming to do the testing necessary. To be honest, you probably need to work on the sales end of it rather than spending your time learning all of the ins and outs of social media advertising. It changes a lot with every Facebook® algorithm change and one minute an ad can work and the next you may get nothing and have to change it.

SECRET #5

Moms on Instagram®

I believe that right now – I am writing this book in the middle of the Covid19 shutdown of 2020- Instagram® has the most potential to reach moms quickly. Don't get me wrong, there are many moms and mom groups on Facebook®. Moms frequent these groups a lot, but most moms are of the age that they are checking Instagram® 6 or more times a day according to SocialMediaToday.com.

There are many mom "influencers" on Instagram®. So that is one potential way to market your business on Instagram®. Influencers, if you are not familiar is the term for someone who people trust on a certain subject or medium, some are celebrities, but many are not know outside of the community that they influence. Contact them and offer products or services for them to review or promote. If you are local to an influencer, make friends and see if there ways you could network with each other.

Another is to start to build up your Instagram® profile. Posting cool pictures is the way to do this, but it can't just be pics of your brand. You might get away with this if you are doing clothing as outfits or something, but people on Instagram® want a high level of creativity and great photos, not sales pitches.

The other thing that is necessary for photos on Instagram® is people. The photos that get the best reaction on Instagram® are those with people in them. Memes do not do as well. So make sure you do photos with cute kids, moms, or of your staff having fun in the pics you post. I was telling an orthodontist that they should take picture of the kid right after they get the braces on – they can't post it without permission, but they can send it to the kid or mom to post it with a #gettingmynewsmile or some appropriate hashtag and tag the Orthodontist's page in it. They should do the same thing on the day they get them off – those are the 2 happiest days the patient has. Dentists could do something similar with a short video of kids brushing their teeth – have the parents film it and tag the office.

One of the things you can to to get pictures is to do a contest. Just like with Facebook®, moms on Instagram® love giveaways. Photo or video contests with a theme do very well. For example if you have a dance or gymnastics studio, you could ask parents to post short videos or photos of their kids having fun dancing – or even a funny mom/kid dance challenge video. Have them tag you with a hashtag that you use for all of your studio posts. The fun challenge videos might not need a prize, but everyone loves to win a prize. It doesn't have to be an expensive one – get a plastic crown (or one from Burger King) for each person in the video and crown the winners, take a picture to display on the wall of the waiting room. Honestly with that sort of publicity the crazier the better, and that sort of "challenge" video will work for almost any kind of business - even doctors, dentists, party businesses etc.

Another feature of both Instagram® and Facebook® that I didn't talk about in the last chapter is "Stories". Stories last only 24 hours on Instagram® or Facebook®. That makes them ideal for time sensitive offers or promotions. Once again you don't want to be spammy, but there is no reason if you have just a couple of items left of something you can't post a picture with the caption "Only 2 Left!!" Or if a deadline is coming for an event or camp, post "Starts Monday" on Friday or Saturday. Limited time offers do really well on that sort of quick format and then you don't have to worry about someone seeing it the next week and calling you when it is over.

Stories can also be utilized to get the word out about your challenge. Say you want to do a new challenge every week. Every day during one week you post the challenge and a new short video or a photo related to it. The next week is a new challenge. As I said at the beginning creativity wins on Instagram®. Once you get to 10,000 followers you can get a link in your stories to use too.

The demographic for Instagram® will be mostly the millennial moms. Short videos and pictures with happy kids or people having fun are the most attractive posts. You can only put one link – in the bio – so make it count too. Start your Instagram® page and get going now. No time like the present, and the sooner you do it, the faster your audience will grow. Be sure to let your clients know about your Instagram® and follow them so that they know to follow your account.

SECRET #6

Moms on Pinterest®

Moms have been known to spend huge amounts of time browsing on Pinterest®. It is usually used as a resource for most. Looking for a new recipe to try? Looking for a kid's craft? Birthday Party ideas? Home decorating? Want to look prettier? Pinterest® is the answer.

The way Pinterest® works is that it is like a bulletin board with all kinds of pictures on it. You can search by category or just look at the most recent "pins". Moms look through the pictures and find something that interests them. They can click on the pin and go to the website that is linked through the pin, or they can choose to post the pin to a "board".
Usually each board is a different subject, but it doesn't have to be. You can have just one board that you put everything on, or you can make a new board for each subject.

Pinterest® photos are usually not of people. They are of things. Food, decorations, fashion, exercise, arts and crafts are the big ones for moms. In order to use Pinterest® to promote organically you can be very creative. The brands in one of the above categories will benefit greatly from using Pinterest® to drive traffic to their website. For instance if you have a business that decorates for parties or caters, it would be very productive to use Pinterest®. Either of these businesses can post pins of their decorations or foods and link back to the page where they have a larger amount of information and get clients from there.

Make sure that any photo or video that you post to Pinterest® is very compelling. You want to have vertical pictures – horizontal pictures will get less space because all of the spaces on Pinterest® are the same width, only the length varies. Pin real estate on Pinterest® is important because you will have to compete with every other pin on the page. You can use text but make it fairly large because it will be small on the page too due to the width.

Examples of how to use Pinterest® to promote a mom or kid oriented business include: A petting zoo could have pictures or short videos of the animals being cute (or interacting with cute kids). These could be put up as pins with little captions or alone with a short write up and a link to the page to book an event. The pictures could also be compiled into a collage or tile pin with the headline being the name of the business or some sort of special offer. Dance studios, gymnastics, tae kwon do and other lesson oriented businesses can do the same thing. Hashtag them too and be sure to follow any of your clients so that they will follow you back. Then they will see anything you post and hopefully pass it on to their friends.

If you have fun pictures on your website you have the option to put a button on the picture so that people visiting your web page can "pin" the picture to their Pinterest® board and it will automatically link back to the original on your site. This is a good place for moonjump pictures and other photo heavy websites to start getting others to help spread the word. You could ask your best clients to go to your website and pin their favorite pictures to their Pinterest® with a short testimonial.

Pinterest® also has a paid option, just like Facebook® and Instagram®, but unlike those, it is a separate entity.
Facebook® and Instagram® are owned by the same company, so you put one ad up and you can run it on both platforms. Pinterest® is owned by a separate company and so has it's own set of ad policies. You should be sure to read through all of the ad policies

on any platform you choose to advertise on, they can be very strict on what you promote, and you can straight up lose your account if they don't like what you are promoting or how you are placing the ads.

SECRET #7

Moms on TikTok®

As with other social media platforms, you will find moms active on TikTok®. I know, TikTok® is for kids and teens right? Not anymore.

TikTok® is a platform where people post videos. TikToks® can be up to 15 seconds long, but users can also connect multiple clips together for up to 60 seconds of total recording. You can also upload longer videos that have been recorded outside of the app itself. It started getting popular with moms when fun dance videos or dashboard lipsync videos were all the rage.

As with the other platforms TikTok® has influencers. There is one mom that does videos of "mom to the rescue", in these she plays the hero to "damsels in distress" - saving her teenage daughter from a guy that is flirting with her. Or jumps in the middle of other funny situations with her kids and their friends. She is not afraid of laughing at herself or embarrassing her kids, though most of the videos seem to be scripted and they are willingly participating.

Other moms do prank videos on their significant others or their kids. Another type of video that you will see moms doing on TikTok® is the "talking head moms". They share advice on parenting and other experiences. This type has some possibilities if you have a mom that really loves your business and wants to do a video and tag you to help you spread the word about it. This is also a good format to use for videos on YouTube® especially when a longer video is warranted.

TikTok® is meant to be funny and short. Some businesses will not be able to utilize it, but some could have a lot of fun and get some great publicity from it. As with Instagram®, TikTok® is a great place to do the video challenges like we talked about earlier. It is also similar to Instagram® in that you get one link in your bio that you can drive traffic through, use hashtags and you can tag people in your posts.

Using the example of the petting zoo earlier, they could use TikTok® to promote their business by showing the animals being cute. There is one lady on TikTok® that films when she feeds her animals and gives them cute voices so that they have a running commentary on their food and interactions with her.

TikTok® is primarily used for entertainment. Unlike the other platforms we have talked about where moms go for friendships, ideas or to brag about their families, it is purely used for fun. Every video has a story. A really fast story sometimes, but a story that makes sense none-the-less. It must be funny, cute or compelling in some way.

Please keep in mind that while TikTok® is meant to be for kids over 13 (as are all of the Social Media platforms) there are a LOT of younger children on TikTok®. If you are targeting moms on TikTok®, keep in mind that if you make the video compelling to a kid, they may be the one's that show mom the video. Children can be fantastic advocates for a business, just look at the McDonald's® Happy Meal® or cereal commercials.

I don't recommend aiming advertising directly at kids, though it is done, I believe it can be unethical. In the case of TikTok® though, if your cute animals are having fun conversations, kids will find that fun and may well introduce your business to moms by showing the video to their parents. Keep your videos G rated and you can have some great word of mouth promotion on TikTok®.

SECRET #8

Moms and Email

Email has gotten a lot of bad press in the past few years because of spam. Plus the social media platforms would really like you to be spending money with them instead of sending free emails out. The truth is, email is still one of the best ways to promote a business today.

According to my research, most moms check their email accounts every day. Some may only check once or twice a week. So while you may not reach moms quickly with email, you can reasonably count on catching her at least one time weekly. Plus, you will catch her when she has time to read and respond to your email because she is in that mode and not rushing to do other things at the time.

The big thing with email is that you don't want to be spam. What makes an email spam? Spam is kind of nebulous in that "anything that the person who owns the account will find annoying or useless". So my suggestion is do not send people information that is not interesting to them or send information too often.

However, one of the best ways to send relevant information on a regular basis is to have a newsletter. It can include special events or promotions that you are holding. Stories of other people like them having fun, relevant information on things that interest them or even just updates on what is going on with your brand. For years I did a calendar of events newsletter every week. The community I lived in had a lot of kids things going on, but until

Facebook® groups dedicated to that were around you had to go many places to find out about the events. Eventually that role was not needed anymore and I started to send links to fun crafts or stories that I had found online as well as movie reviews done by kids.

The best way to use an email list is to get permission from the person to send them emails. You can do this any number of ways. You can have a newsletter sign-up form on your website, if you have a brick and mortar location or a booth somewhere, you can ask them to sign up in person, or you can send an initial email to them asking them to opt in to a link you send them in the email. Most likely they will be fine with it if they like doing business with you or want to in the future.

Mail Chimp is a free service for sending emails until you get 2000 subscribers, after that they have a paid service. There are several other options if you want to pay for a service: Aweber and Constant Contact are 2 that I am familiar with. I have been using Mail Chimp for many years though and they have been great. If you already have an email list or get people to sign up in person, you can put the emails and names in a spreadsheet, save it as a .csv file and upload it to start your list there.

Do not neglect getting a good email list. The reason I say this is you own that information. No matter what happens to your social media accounts – yes sometimes they will get shut down for no reason and you will have to work to get them back – or something else happens. You will always have the email connections. Most people keep emails for a very long time too, it is not unusual for an email to be active for years. Keep in touch with your clients and they will be more likely to return and do business with you again too.

The nice thing about email is that you can send as much information as you like for no extra charge. You can drive traffic to your website or other social media if you want. You can ask the recipient to reply back or tell them about something fantastic you have to offer that you know they will want. It is very useful to have the ability to speak directly to your clients and to be honest they will appreciate the personal attention you can give them via emails.

SECRET #9

Mom Loyalty Programs

What is a loyalty program? This is a way to recognize moms for staying loyal to your business, keep them coming back and to even encourage them to come back if they are new.

Loyalty programs are rewards, they are a great way to personalize your customer service and also to softly market to them.

The ways that loyalty programs are put into place can be very different. Some examples of loyalty programs that we are all familiar with are punch cards or stamp cards. Subway had a loyalty program for years, you would take their little card in and have it stamped and after 10 stamps you would get a free six inch sub sandwich. Hair salons sometimes do this, have 9 haircuts and your tenth is free.

This is not the only way to do a loyalty program by any stretch though. More recent loyalty programs are often done with text messaging. Sonic® has a program where you sign up and receive alert texts for discounts or free items to get you to come to their store and mention the text you get the reward. This appears to be a loss leader strategy. Many other fast food restaurants have their own apps where you have them scan the app on your phone and you get points to redeem on future orders.

Loyalty programs can be used by more than hair salons and restaurants, but often they are not. Some mom specific loyalty programs include:

- **Once Upon a Child**® – a children's resale store has a stamp card where you get a free item after 10 purchases.
- **BabyList**® – a wish list registration for moms online lets its users save money and get funds from others for their child's future education. Can't think of a better way to build emotional attachment among users than with a practical approach like this.
- **ChildrensPlace**® - a kid's clothing company also has after every dollar spent, they reward customers with 2 points. Furthermore, after shopping moms collect 100 points, they're rewarded with a $5 coupon to use toward their next purchase. And on top of the savings incentives, they have a smart birthday perk which gives moms a 20% discount around their child's birthday.
- **Peek Kids Clothing**® – another kid's clothing retailer offers rewards to moms if they 1) send an invitation to a friend, 2) the invited friend registers on their site, 3) this friend makes a purchase and 4) loyalty members submit new product reviews on their site.

Birthday offers are an excellent way to implement a rewards program. There was a burger place in the city I used to live in that would send a post card to my husband every year for his birthday. It included a free birthday meal for the birthday boy/girl and expired a month after his birthday. Every year he chose to go to that restaurant to celebrate and usually we took our family of 4 and his 2 parents. That was 5 meals purchased for the cost of 1 post card and 1 meal. How many families do you think took them up on that offer and brought others with them?

According to Makesbridge®, newsletters that remind moms about birthday offers have on average, an 83% open rate. Impressive! So at the very minimum you should consider starting a rewards program for your clients. Everyone loves free or discounted things and as with other types of marketing it doesn't necessarily need to be expensive.

Emails, text messages and social media posts are very useful for Secrets of getting these offers out to your customers. It is also a good pretext to get people to sign up to your email list.

SECRET #10

Events for Moms

Holding events for moms are one of the best and quickest ways to build relationships with your clients. It will also draw new moms to your brand and encourage your loyal moms to invite others to give you a chance. Moms are very hungry for other adult company and they love to take their kids to hang out with other kids too. If you were to hold an event for moms and kids every month it would likely be very well attended.

Your events will need to be a lot of fun and you will need to do publicity to make any event successful. Places that have play equipment, moonjumps or party businesses will, of course, be some of the most successful with this.

Museums, zoos and aquariums can use events like this yearly to grow membership rolls. Do an event, invite tons of moms and offer a special offer for signing up for a membership. This can be a discount or even a special perk for them or their kids.

Restaurants with kids areas will find these to be a great way to encourage parents to patronize them. As a restaurant you can hold a weekly or monthly "kids eat free" or "kids eat half off" (usually done with a buy an adult meal for each child).

You can even use that in combination with your rewards program and hold an event on a day that is usually very slow. Make sure to get them to sign up for your birthday club and rewards program while they are at your event! You can monetize it by having vendors at the event and charging them $10 or $20 for a table. There are a lot of moms that have side hustle businesses that love low cost opportunities to promote during events like those.

For publicity you can send out press releases, get added to event calendars locally and be sure to create an event on Facebook® and share it everywhere. You can use a photo or video and put the details on other social media as well.

Be sure to share to the "garage sale" groups on Facebook® and send requests to share your event on mom groups. Often if the event is free they will allow you to share it or they will promote it for you. If you run across one that won't ask them if they want to be a sponsor and give them a booth or tell them they can put a banner up at the event.

Trade and promoting other businesses during your event is a great way to get help from other businesses that moms frequent. You can ask a local pizza place that does parties to donate some pizzas, or a bakery to give you some snacks in return for publicity for their businesses.

For a very special event talk to a local photographer about taking pictures of your event and let them hand out cards or coupons for their services. Some photographers will even set up a "mini" session at the event where they offer pictures for sale to the parents. Magicians or balloon artists are also good people to collaborate with to make an awesome event. You may want to only do this yearly at this scale, but even dentists and doctors etc. can use events like these to grow their businesses.

We used to hold a "Mama's Club Play Group" event monthly at a different business every time. We asked that the event was free – they could sell whatever they wanted and memberships were a very successful promotion at these events. We also asked them to provide snacks and drinks for the kids. That was their only expense. We had usually 4 or 5 vendors and typically had 10 or

12 moms show up with their kids. One time we had 50 moms show up with their kids – it was crazy! We did all of the publicity and held them at all kinds of locations including 3 different moonjump places, Rainbow Play Stations®, a gymnastics gym, an athletic club and others.

Another type of event that I want to mention is arts and craft shows. Moms love to go to events where they can shop.
These are great events for places that have a separate room to utilize, but you can use it to just get people into your shop too. I have seen moonwalk places, art studios, restaurants, even a bar use this for an event. The best time to do this is during the holiday season.

Lastly, there are often Health, Back to School and Summer Camp fairs that are held to reach out to moms. They will offer a place for businesses to rent a booth and provide information and value to the moms that attend the fairs.

Many moms will make a day of attending these fairs with their families or close friends. At these booths you want to make sure you are open and friendly as they visit your booth. I haven't seen it very often, but I really suggest you have something that will give the kids a chance to do something to keep their attention while you visit with the moms. Coloring pages (with washable crayons or markers), stamps or another quick craft are good choices and moms really appreciate the extra effort made to keep the kids busy.

Note: During and after Covid19 we are having many events canceled, so we will see a huge benefit from online events. Most moms are tired of webinars and regular Zoom® calls though, so be creative. We will need to find a way to incorporate the energy, excitement and connections that are what events are all about. Recently, I ran across some great ideas to make this happen. Some of the things to include are swag, breakout rooms to chat with other participants or vendors and lots of interaction with the hosts of the events. Think outside of the box and be innovative to reach moms with these sorts of events.

SECRET #11

Mom groups, print and other options

We talked a little about mom groups in previous chapters, but the one thing that moms really seek out is other moms. They are looking for other adults that have the same problems that they do, who will socialize and not mind children running around. In order to fulfill this objective they turn to mom groups and if there are none, they will create their own.

You will find these groups called various things and some are even run by non-profits. MOPS®, playgroups, park groups and church sponsored play days are all included in these social gatherings. These groups are usually very informal, but I have been to some that had more direct oversight and where they sometimes had dentists pass out toothbrushes. Some even brought in guests sometimes to talk with the moms about their businesses benefiting the families.

There are also many print publications local and national that are aimed at moms and parents. Kids are one place, as I have said before, where parents are willing to spend lots of money. Moms like to keep up to date on what is available to do locally and get ideas for activities to do with the kids out and at home. Advertising in these publications is really a hidden gem. They get passed around among the moms and are even sought out each time they are published. National print is one place that you can use to get the word out about products and services available.

Local publications are overlooked as an option for larger businesses, so the smaller local businesses have a great opportunity to reach a very targeted local market for not very much investment. There is tremendous staying power for print advertising. I have not distributed the publication that I had for almost 2 years and I still occasionally get calls to advertise or to find a local business now.

Often these publications have more than just the print opportunities too. Many have online groups, email lists and web resources that can be very economical in order to reach a truly interested and targeted audience. Moms are interested in what is being given to them so it breaks through the noise of junk mail and online ads that people tend to ignore.

Fliers are also a good investment. Post cards are easy to pass out and moms will toss them into their purse or car and run across them more than once, keeping you top of mind. Print coupons and special offers on them or just use enticing copy to get your message across. Be sure to use lots of colorful pictures of cute kids (this goes for any ads that you do).

Fliers can be handed out at events and sometimes schools or preschools will allow them to be left on the counters of the school or sent home in backpacks. I will caution you that sending things home in backpacks may not be the greatest thing you can do to reach moms. The stuff in backpacks is like junk mail. It just goes straight in the trash unless it needs a signature.

Mommy blogs have gained a huge following in the past few years too. Many have lots of traffic and do not charge much in order to reach out to their mom audiences. They also have huge email lists a lot of times and for a small fee will allow you to send "email blasts". Some have opportunities for relevant brands to sponsor their blogs or events that they hold. These audiences are very loyal and working with these mommy bloggers is akin to working with influencers. It is a great place to reach out to moms.

Keep your eyes open, there are often sponsorship opportunities where you can call attention to your brand. Some grocery stores allow booths outside and these can be very effective too. Be careful to keep to your budget with sponsorships and only sponsor things or places that will benefit your brand significantly if you want a good R.O.I. If you are a business that caters to elementary school children, you might pass on sponsoring the high school calendar. Stick with your niche and best demographic. If you want to sponsor an organization that is not your target, you can still support them, but don't use your marketing budget for it.

Think out of the box too. I know of a photographer that got many, many customers because she would take pictures of the kids or grandkids of local restaurant and business owners, then she would have those pictures framed nicely and hung in the business' location with her card and number attached. The photos were so cute that the clients of that business would call and set up appointments just on that promotion.

Another photographer that specialized in newborns had some very nice baby pictures framed and gave them to the local OBGYN offices to hang as decorations with her card attached. She had lots of business from those partnerships.

What can you do to think out of the box? What can you offer a business to give them something special that will give you referrals back? If you have a bakery, maybe you go to a local credit union and offer to give them a plate of cookies or cake to do a customer appreciation for their clients if they will put up a sign saying who donated the sweets. Maybe you have a pizza place and you offer to give them a discount if a local party place will serve your pizza at the parties and pass out your business coupon to the moms at the party so they order from you later. If you have a kids dental office, maybe you get a daycare to put a cup with toothbrushes to give away on their counter with your name on it. Or work a referral deal with a local pediatrician to recommend each other to your patients. Many businesses are used to referral situations, orthodontists get referrals from dentist all the time, there is no reason that other family friendly businesses can't do the same thing.

SECRET #12

Enticements and Offers for Moms

Now that you know where moms are and what platforms you can use to reach them. What are the best ways to incentivize them to patronize your business?

Offers are important and work well. Coupons, buy one get one (BOGO) and discount packages are very popular. However, incentives don't have to be monetary. You should consider what you offer to moms and their kids in your regular brand values.

Is your business inviting and fun? Is the staff friendly and knowledgeable? Or is is run down and dirty? Are your staff surly and unhelpful? If you can find out what the customer sees. Put up some cameras or have a mystery shopper come in to evaluate. Even call to find out how the phone is answered. All of those things matter.

I have to tell you that nothing will run a mom off faster than a dirty store. You can have a very simple, even bare bones establishment and they will still come and bring their children if it is clean and you provide value with your entertainment, services or products. I have literally seen a painted cinderblock dance studio with a basic dance floor and mirrors be extraordinarily successful because of the quality and the caring of the dance teachers. I have seen photography studios in a home garage conversion be the most popular place to get photos in town because the photographer worked with the kids and got fantastic photos. Both places not only offered great value, but were super clean because the people running them were almost fanatical about it.

I know many moms that hate going to certain stores and restaurants with indoor playscapes because they are not clean – even pre-Covid19. Many will stick to drive thru because their kids love the food, but they hate the fact that there are a lot of germs there. Other places are super popular because they keep their equipment clean and the moms see them doing it.

Note: This is going to be especially important to moms as we come out of the Covid19 shutdown. Moms are already freaked out because of the fear that has been spread everywhere, they will be demanding cleanliness above all after businesses open again, perhaps for years to come.

So if you have high chairs, scrub them down. If you have a play area, be seen cleaning it between uses. Also, be careful of the products that you use on those items, I have seen kids get chemical burns from some products. You definitely do not want that to happen. Word gets around among mothers. Both good and bad will be spread quickly through the networks, but bad hygiene spreads fastest.

Beyond cleanliness, safety and value are the keys to making a great impression and having success in the mom market. Implement your loyalty program and try to personalize the experience of each customer. Talk to them, but don't try to sell them. If you are friendly and helpful they will appreciate it, but no one wants to feel pressured. Even if they say, "I am just looking", make small talk – ask them about their kids etc. Moms like it when they get to talk to other adults, and will appreciate your business for putting them at ease while they visit you.

If you want to take advantage of the mom networks then you should also consider setting up a formalized referral system. Moms get an incentive for sending or bringing other moms to your business. Gyms do this all of the time with "bring a friend" promotions. Find a way to give your moms a reward of some kind if they send another mom that purchases something – and be sure to follow up with the referrer and thank them.

You can set up a photo booth or wall decoration of some sort to get moms to take selfies or kid pics that they can share on their social media accounts – be sure your logo or brand name is visible. There was a mall near me one time that did that and called it their "selfie zone". It worked really well and they got tons of free press on social media.

SECRET #13

Moms and Your Website

We haven't talked about your website in all of this. I am a huge believer in the power of a website for a small business. Your website is essential in this age of the internet. Your website is one of the few things you have complete control over. You can carefully craft the message you use to portray your business on that medium and continually put more and more relevant content up there to grow the number of people that visit your site (traffic).

Your website is the equivalent of a picture window on Main Street in the past. People use it to check out what you have before they decide to do business with you or not. Make sure you have a website to be one of your first lines of contact to new clients. It can also be helpful in client retention depending upon what you do with it. Almost every buyer journey these days starts with a search online. We don't even think about it, we look up products, locations, hours, services and information about everything that we are even remotely interested in buying.

It can be very inexpensive to build a website. You can hire someone to do it for you or you can do it yourself. Wix and Weebly are extremely affordable and so is Wordpress, though it is a bit more complex to build one there. Your website should include easy to navigate pages, don't be tempted to use cute titles for your pages, just make it easy to use. Keep user experience (UX) in mind for everything you put up on the site. You can use your creativity for your information and for your images.

Other than using a website as the "face" online of your business, there are several reasons to have a great website. We talked about Facebook®, Instagram®, Pinterest ® and TikTok® earlier in this book as well as events and other means to reach out to moms, right? In every one of those chapters I spoke about using links for people to find out more about you. If you don't have a website, where are you driving that mom traffic to? You can utilize each and every channel in this book to your advantage by being intentional about how you use your website.

Events can be listed on your website and you can even put them in a slide on the front page to publicize them. If you are sending traffic from Pinterest, you probably want to send the link to a specific blog page or article. You can write blog posts and share them on Facebook or Instagram and you can have a video page and put quick videos up about things that will interest your clients too. And don't forget the opportunity to use your website to get people to sign up on your email list so that you can reach out to them directly. Your website can be used much more flexibly and more effectively than just having a Facebook business page, so don't fall into that trap.

Many argue that they don't need a website, because they can't contact people that visit their website. It is true that only about 2% of website visitors will ever contact you directly. More moms may sign up for your email list, if your content is enticing, but the percentage is still low – around 4-5%. Now there is a software platform which has recently become affordable, that you can use to actually get information about the people who visit your website. (Previously it has only been affordable for very large businesses.) It can provide you the name and email (more information if you are a business to business brand), so that you can either reach out directly, or use paid advertising to target those exact people or a wider audience that mirrors those people. And just like the email list, with this company's product you actually own the information so you can use it in any number of ways to generate more revenue for your brand.

So my advice to you is make sure your current website is on point to attract your mom audience and if it is not, or you don't have one, get it done. Start linking your social media to the relevant pages on your website and work on your content. Get your traffic up by using some or all of the techniques in this book and then take a look at the contact platform I mentioned. If you are interested in finding out more about that software just go to my website www.markettomoms.com and there will be more information and a link to the site there.

Your website is a vital part of your business in this current economy and culture, do not neglect the impact it can have on your business. I didn't mention it, but you can also use it to have people sign up for events, classes or book parties. You can link it to a merchant account or PayPal® and they can even do a deposit or pay online. There is so much you can do with your website that it is a serious oversight to not employ it in your business.

SECRET #14

The Mom Market and Your Brand

Moms are a terrific niche to be in for many businesses. There is a lot of profit to be made while providing service to moms. They appreciate value and are willing to spend money on their children, even skimping on themselves to do it.

Think about it. Every kid in the area has a birthday each year, they all need new clothes for school, and usually at the beginning of summer too. They have to go to the dentist, doctor and get haircuts more than once a year. Parents are willing to spend money on entertainment and restaurants on a regular basis and on lessons almost year round. Camps, sports and daycares are large expenditures. There is so much opportunity to do business with moms.

That doesn't even include fashion, gyms, hair and nails etc. for the moms themselves. As well as the home repairs, electronics, utilities, pets and decorations that they are usually in charge of arranging for the family. Do not underestimate the influence that mom has, usually around 83% of buying decisions are done by moms for their families.

Think out of the box to reach that mom audience. Know what they want and who your ideal mom profile is, so that you can effectively and economically reach out to bring them into your business. It will be worth it.

There is more information on marketing to moms and in general on my website www.marketomoms.com please check it out if you are interested in learning more about this subject.

I wish you much success and joy in working with your mom clients. Please reach out with your stories – I would love to hear them!

www.ingramcontent.com/pod-product-compliance
Lightning Source LLC
Chambersburg PA
CBHW050305220526

45465CB00002B/832